language skills

Writing in Action

level **b**

LOYOLAPRESS.

Managing Editor	Kim Mason
Production Manager	Mary Bowers
Editors	Sandy Hazel, Jan Marcus, Margaret O'Leary
Production Staff	Phyllis Martinez, Kari Nicholls, Steve Straus
Interior Design	Mary Bowers

Acknowledgments

Grateful acknowledgment is made to the following authors, agents, and publishers for the use of copyrighted material. Every effort has been made to trace the ownership of all copyrighted material and to secure the necessary permissions to reprint these selections. Any errors or omissions are unintentional and will be corrected in future printings.

AMBER BROWN GOES FOURTH, copyright © 1995 by Paula Danziger. Published by G.P. Putnam's Sons.

THE IROQUOIS: A FIRST AMERICANS BOOK, copyright © 1995 by Virginia Driving Hawk Sneve. Published by Holiday House, Inc.

Images copyright © Photodisc 1997.

ISBN 0-8294-1003-1

©1997 Loyola Press
3441 N. Ashland Avenue
Chicago, Illinois 60657

Pages 52-68 © 2002 K12 Inc.

Printed in the United States of America

1 2 3 4 5 6   2 1 0 9 8 7

WRITING A BOOK REPORT

LESSON 1

PREWRITING: Talking About the Book Report

Reading a book is like climbing into a time machine. You can travel back to the time of dinosaurs or of cowboys. You can read about the future of living in outer space. A book might take you to another neighborhood with people like you. You can even travel to imaginary times and places.

If you're like most people, you'll want to tell someone about your trip when you get back. That's one reason for writing a book report. It's a way to share what happened.

Here are some reasons for writing book reports. Which ones do you think are most important? Mark your choices with an X.

1. Book reports let me tell what I liked or didn't like about a book. ☐

2. They make me think more carefully about what I am reading. ☐

3. They help my family know what kind of books I like. ☐

4. They give me a chance to improve my writing. ☐

5. They help my friends learn about books they might not have read yet. ☐

If you checked all five reasons, you're right! *All* the reasons are important.

What Is a Book Report?

Let's look at these two words: *book* and *report*. You know what a book is. And you probably know about some other kinds of reports. Finish the following sentences:

1. A news report tells about _____ .

2. A science report tells about _____ .

3. A book report tells about _____ .

   What three words are in every one of the sentences you just read?

   _____   _____   _____

Yes! A REPORT is a piece of writing that TELLS ABOUT something. It gives facts and information.

WRITER'S WORKSHOP

A BOOK REPORT is a piece of writing that tells about a book.

Choosing a Book

To enjoy writing your book report, choose a book that interests you. These sentences will help you decide what kind of book you enjoy most. Put a check mark by each statement you agree with. If you enjoy something we didn't think of, write it in the last space.

☐ I like make-believe stories about unusual people and places.

☐ I like stories about people my own age who think and feel as I do.

☐ I like mysteries or scary stories.

☐ I like stories about outer space.

☐ I like stories about dragons and other imaginary creatures.

☐ I like to know about real adventures that people have had.

☐ I like to know about people who lived in the past.

☐ I like to know about subjects from science (such as rocks, whales, or airplanes).

☐ I am a sports fan. My favorite player is _____

_____ .

☐ I like to learn more about my hobby, which is _____

_____ .

☐ _____

_____

✓ Now it's time to choose a book! No matter what you like best, someone has written an interesting book about it. Your librarian can help you find it in your library.

PREWRITING: Answering Questions About Your Book

By now, you've read the book for your report. Now it's time to TELL ABOUT the book you read. Here is a form to help you decide what you want to say. First, finish these sentences:

The title of the book I read is _____ .

It was written by _____ .

Next, answer these questions with "yes" or "no."

A. What kind of book is it?

an informational book? _____   about a science subject? _____

a book of poems?   _____   a make-believe story?   _____

a play or script?   _____   a true adventure story? _____

Is it something else? What? _____

B. If it is a make-believe story, is it a special kind of story?

a mystery? _____

a story from the past? _____

a family story? _____

an adventure story? _____

a story about someone like you and your friends? _____

another kind of story? What kind? _____

C. What special things did I enjoy about the book?

Is it sad? _____ funny? _____ scary? _____

exciting? _____ full of information? _____

Does it keep you guessing? _____

Are the people in the book fun to know? _____

Does it happen in an unusual place? _____

Does the book teach a lesson? _____

D. What did I like best about the book? _____

_____

_____

E. Do I think my friends should read this book? Why? _____

_____

_____

✓ Choose one of the questions in Part C that you answered "yes." Write an

example from the story that explains your answer. _____

_____

_____

_____

_____

_____

PREWRITING: Writing a Summary

One important part of a book report is called a SUMMARY. A summary is a short way of telling what is in a book. It includes only the most important facts or events (things that happen).

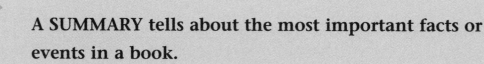

WRITER'S WORKSHOP

A SUMMARY tells about the most important facts or events in a book.

Here are three steps you can follow to write a summary:

1. Make a list of the main facts or events in the book.
2. Choose the most important ones. Cross out the others.
3. Write a paragraph about the most important facts or events.

Making a List

If your book is nonfiction, make your list from the names of chapters. If the book has no chapters, look for headings. You might just ask yourself, "What are the important parts of the book that I want to tell about?"

Here is part of a sample list from an informational book. The book is *The Iroquois* by Virginia Driving Hawk Sneve.

1. The Iroquois League
2. Men
3. Women
4. Children
5. The Iroquois Today

If your book is fiction, list the events that happened at the beginning, in the middle, and at the end of the story. Here is a list of things that happened in a book called *Amber Brown Goes Fourth* by Paula Danziger.

1. Amber Brown's best friend Justin has moved, so she needs a new one.

2. Hannah Burton needs a best friend, too, but she's bossy and mean.

3. Brandi Colwin, a new girl last year, returns to class.

4. Amber thinks Brandi will make a good friend.

5. When Amber compares Justin to Brandi, Brandi gets mad.

6. Amber and Brandi get the giggles and get detention together.

7. Amber and Brandi do fun things together.

8. Brandi tells Amber how hard it was to make friends as a new kid in school.

9. They decide to be nice to any new kids, even if they become best friends.

✓ Now you try it. Use the space below to make a list of the main parts of the book you read.

_____

_____

_____

_____

_____

_____

_____

_____

Choosing the Most Important Parts

The next step is to choose the parts that you want to write about in your report. Look at your list again and cross out items that could be left out. Be sure to keep all the facts and events that are needed to understand the book. Don't cross out too many.

Writing the Summary

The last step is to write one or more paragraphs, using the list you've made. Give facts from the book. Add details to make the paragraphs interesting. Here is a summary paragraph about the Iroquois. Look again at the list on page 6. What main parts of the book are described?

> Iroquois men were skilled hunters. They made all their tools and weapons. They used trees and branches to make spears, bowls, spoons, and canoes. Iroquois women planted crops and prepared food. They sewed clothes and made baskets for gathering roots and plants. Both men and women also found time to play games.

☑ Turn back to the list you made on page 7. On your own sheet of paper, write one or more paragraphs about your book. When you're finished, put your paper in your writing folder or other safe place. These paragraphs will be the summary for your book report.

PREWRITING: Writing Good Paragraphs

Paragraphs with facts have a MAIN IDEA. It is what the paragraph is about. A TOPIC SENTENCE presents the main idea of the paragraph to the reader. It is like the announcer of a TV program. Sometimes a paragraph does not have a topic sentence. But a paragraph always has a main idea.

A paragraph about facts has a MAIN IDEA.
The TOPIC SENTENCE tells the main idea of
the paragraph.

A. Underline the topic sentence in each paragraph below. Then circle a) or b) to complete the sentence under each paragraph.

   The Iroquois were known as the "people of the longhouse." They lived in long, rectangular houses. Usually five families lived in a longhouse. Each family had a section with its own fire pit and hearth.

1. The main idea of this paragraph is
   a) what the longhouse was like
   b) where the Iroquois lived

Children learned how to do things by watching and listening to adults. Young girls sewed clothes for their cornhusk dolls. They watched the women cook. Young boys played with bows and arrows and pretended to hunt. At night they listened to stories of Iroquois history and customs.

2. The main idea of this paragraph is

   a) what kinds of games children played

   b) how children learned to do things

B. Here is a paragraph that does *not* have a topic sentence. Read the paragraph. Circle a) or b) to identify which is the best topic sentence.

Five Iroquois tribes lived in what is now the state of New York. These tribes often fought with each other. One day, a man named Peacemaker convinced the tribes to work together. They formed the Iroquois League. The Five Nations of the league stopped fighting among themselves and helped each other.

The best topic sentence is

a) A man named Peacemaker was an Iroquois warrior.

b) Five Iroquois tribes formed the Iroquois League.

✓ Look at the summary paragraphs you wrote. Did you write a summary of a nonfiction, informational book? If so, make sure each of your paragraphs has a main idea. Do you need to add topic sentences? If you wrote about a fictional story, are the events in the proper order?

LESSON 5

DRAFTING: Beginning to Write

Here is a riddle for you: How is a book report like a dog? Answer: each has a beginning, a middle, and an ending!

The beginning of a book report is called the INTRODUCTION. The middle of a book report is called the BODY. The ending is called the CONCLUSION.

A book report has an INTRODUCTION, a BODY, and a CONCLUSION.

Guess what? You've already written part of your book report. The summary you wrote in Lesson 3 will be the body of your book report. Most of the other information you need is in your answers to the questions on pages 4 and 5.

Planning Your Introduction

The beginning of your book report is called its introduction. Make it as strong and interesting as you can. An introduction has two important jobs.

1. It should get the reader's attention. Maybe you could describe something exciting that happened in the book. Or begin with the part you liked best about the book. Jot down your idea for an interesting beginning at the top of page 12.

_____

_____

_____

_____

_____

2. Your introduction must give the title of the book and the author's name. You should also tell what kind of book the author has written. Write the information here:

Name of book _____

Name of author _____

Kind of book _____

WRITER'S WORKSHOP

The INTRODUCTION to a book report includes the name of the book and its author. The introduction also should get the reader's attention.

A. Here is a sample introduction for a book report:

   Josh Allen is a twelve-year-old boy who has a problem. He always gets blamed for things he didn't do. His brother gets all the attention, and Josh is upset.

Does this introduction get the reader's attention? _____

But what is missing? _____

B. Now read this introduction:

   Boys turn into TV sets and girls eat whales in a book of poems by Shel Silverstein. The book is called *Where the Sidewalk Ends*. Some of the poems are funny and some make us think. All of them are happy.

Does this introduction get the reader's attention? _____

Does it tell the author, title, and kind of book? _____

C. Read the paragraph above again. Underline the sentence that gets the reader's attention. Draw a circle around the name of the book. Draw a box around the name of the author. Put brackets [ ] around the words that tell the kind of book.

Writing Your Introduction

Think of the introduction you are writing as a first draft. Don't worry too much about spelling or other errors. You can fix them later. The purpose of a first draft is to get your ideas down on paper.

✓ Write an introduction for your book report on the lines below. Look back to pages 4-5 to get ideas for your introduction. Include an interesting beginning to get the reader's attention. Remember to include the author's name, the title of the book, and the kind of book. Underline the name of the book.

_____

_____

_____

_____

_____

_____

DRAFTING: Writing the Body of Your Book Report

What part of a dog is the longest? Its body, right? The same thing is true of a book report. The body of a book report is longer than its other parts.

The summary you wrote in Lesson 3 will be the body of your book report. The body may have one, two, or even three paragraphs.

WRITER'S WORKSHOP

> The BODY of a book report is a summary of the book.
> It also includes details and examples.

To make your book report interesting, add details and examples.

You read a list of things that happened in the book *Amber Brown Goes Fourth*. Look back on page 7 if you need to. Here is one event: Hannah Burton needs a best friend, too, but she's bossy and mean.

A. Below are the sentences from the book report that tell what happens when Amber goes to school. Underline each detail or example the writer of the book report has added.

At school, Amber discovers that Hannah Burton and Brandi Colwin aren't best friends anymore. Hannah needs a best friend, but she is bossy and mean. Amber thinks she is a monster.

B. Add some details or examples to the body of your book report. Look through your book again to help you remember. Use the rest of this page to list some details and examples you could add.

1. Fact or event: _____

   Details or examples: _____

   _____

   _____

   _____

2. Fact or event: _____

   Details or examples: _____

   _____

   _____

   _____

3. Fact or event: _____

   Details or examples: _____

   _____

   _____

   _____

☑ Copy the introduction you wrote on page 13 on another sheet of paper. Then write the body of your book report following it. Use the summary you wrote earlier, adding some details or examples.

DRAFTING: Writing a Conclusion

What Should a Conclusion Do?

Your book report should have a strong ending. If it doesn't, your readers may think you just got tired and stopped writing. Your report will be like a dog without a tail.

Here are some questions you should answer in your ending:

1. What did you like (or dislike) about the book?
2. What kind of reader do you think would enjoy the book?

Do the examples below answer those questions? Underline the words that tell why the writer of the report liked the book. Put brackets [ ] around the words that tell what kind of reader would enjoy the book.

A. *Where the Sidewalk Ends* is a funny book. The poems made me laugh, and I liked the drawings. The book begins by saying, "If you are a dreamer, come in." Are you a dreamer? If you are, you will like this book.

B. In this story, Amber learns that being best friends doesn't always happen right away. It takes time. She also learns that new kids in class can make good friends. I like the book because Amber and Brandi act like real kids. If you have a friend who has moved away, or if you have been a new kid in school, you will like this book. You probably feel the same way that Amber and Brandi do.

Writing the Conclusion

WRITER'S WORKSHOP

The CONCLUSION of a book report tells why the writer of the report liked or disliked the book. It also tells what kind of reader would like the book.

☑ Now write the conclusion for your book report on your first draft. You can use information from your work sheet on page 5. Be sure to tell why you liked or disliked the book. Also tell what kind of reader you think would enjoy the book. Finally, tell what you think that person would enjoy about the book.

REVISING: Improving Your Report

Making It Better

Congratulations! You have written a complete draft of your book report. Gather all the parts you have written so far. Put them in this order:

1. Introduction
2. Body (your summary with added details and examples)
3. Conclusion

When writers finish their first draft, they know that the work is not over. Now it is time to make the writing even better.

When their first draft is finished, writers begin to REVISE (change and improve) their report.

Today you will revise by checking to see if your introduction, body, and conclusion all do their jobs well. In later lessons you will choose better words and check for correct spelling, grammar, and punctuation.

Sometimes it's not easy to make changes to your own writing. You might read your draft and think, "It's fine. It makes sense to me. It's good enough."

But remember, you are not writing this report for you. You are writing it for other people to read. You want your readers to learn something when they read your report. You want them to enjoy reading it. That is why you revise your draft. By revising, you can go from "good enough" to "great!"

Here are two versions of a paragraph from a student's book report about *The Hundred Dresses*, by Eleanor Estes. The first version is the draft. The second version is the revision. Read both. Then tell what changes the writer made to improve the draft.

Wanda does have one hundred dresses. She drew them. Her drawings win her the art medal at school. Wanda Petronski is poor and different. Peggy and Maddie make fun of her when she says she has one hundred dresses. I would never be mean like that, even if someone was really strange and poor.

Revision:

Wanda Petronski is poor and different, and Peggy and Maddie make fun of her when she says she has one hundred dresses. They know Wanda is too poor to have all those dresses because she wears a faded blue dress. But Wanda does have one hundred dresses. She drew them. Her drawings win her the art medal at school.

Revising Your Draft

Use these checklists to help you decide where your draft needs revising. Even if you check "Yes" for everything, try to change one thing from each section to make the report better.

Introduction   Yes   No

Does my introduction give the title of the book?   ☐   ☐

Does my introduction name the author?   ☐   ☐

Does my introduction catch the reader's attention?   ☐   ☐

Body

Does the body of my report give a summary of the book?   ☐   ☐

Have I written events in the order in which they happened?   ☐   ☐

Is each of the paragraphs about only one main idea?   ☐   ☐

Does each paragraph have a topic sentence that tells what the
paragraph is about?   ☐   ☐

Does each paragraph tell interesting details and examples?   ☐   ☐

Conclusion

Does the conclusion tell why I liked the book?   ☐   ☐

Does it tell why someone else should read the book?   ☐   ☐

REVISING: Improving Your Sentences

What is wrong with the paragraph below?

Amelia wanted to build a flying machine and she got lumber and nails and built one and put one end of the track in a barn window and the other end on the ground. She rode on it and ran into her grandma.

The problem with this paragraph is _____

_____ .

Yes! Its sentences are all hooked together with "ands." The word "and" is a CONJUNCTION. A conjunction is a word that joins two thoughts together in one sentence.

But "and" is just one conjunction. There are many others. Your writing will be clearer and more interesting if you choose the conjunction that fits each sentence best. Here are some examples:

Jenny was tired, **and** she went to bed.

Jenny was tired, **so** she went to bed.

In that sentence, **and** tells us only that the two thoughts are connected. **So** tells us *in what way* the thoughts are connected. **So** tells us that the first part of the sentence gives the *reason* for the second part.

Jimmy stood up for Amelia, **and** she liked him better.

After Jimmy stood up for Amelia, she liked him better.

After tells us *when* Amelia liked Jimmy better.

Using the Best Conjunction

Write a conjunction in each blank below. Use as many different conjunctions as you can. You may choose conjunctions from this list:

then but so when after because

1. Amelia wanted to go on a trip with her father, _____ she couldn't.

2. Grandma thought that Amelia should play with dolls _____ she was a girl.

3. _____ her parents left, Amelia felt sad.

4. Amelia wanted to build a flying machine, _____ she got lumber and nails.

5. She built one. _____ she put one end in a barn window and the other end on the ground.

6. _____ she rode the flying machine, she ran into her grandma.

7. Amelia could have been in trouble, _____ Jimmy took the blame.

8. _____ Jimmy stood up for Amelia, she liked him better.

WRITER'S WORKSHOP

Use the CONJUNCTION that makes the meaning of each sentence clearest.

☑ Read the first draft of your book report. Have you joined too many sentences together with "and"? If you have, choose conjunctions that make the meaning of your sentences clearer.

Another Sentence Problem: Choppiness

Here is another paragraph that has a sentence problem. Can you tell what the problem is?

Not all dinosaurs were huge. Many dinosaurs were very large. Some were small. Some were as small as chickens. They could run fast.

Did you say that the sentences were too short and choppy? See if you can fix the problem. Combine three of the sentences into one sentence. The clues under each blank will give you some help.

Many dinosaurs were very large, _____ some were small
(use a conjunction)

_____ .
(how small?)

Here are some more sentences for you to combine. The questions under the blanks will give you some hints.

1. Amelia lived on a farm. The farm was in Kansas.

   Amelia lived on a farm _____ .
   (where?)

2. Amelia got wheels from roller skates. The roller skates were old.
   They were rusty.

   Amelia got wheels from _____ , _____ roller skates.
   (what kind of?)

3. Grandma was surprised. She was angry.

   Grandma was surprised _____ angry.
   (use a conjunction)

✔ Look at the first draft of your book report again. Does it have too many short sentences?

REVISING: Improving Your Word Choices

1. The car went up a mountain road.

2. The old clunker struggled up the mountain road.

Which sentence is more interesting? Why? Here are some ways to make your writing more fun for both you and your readers.

Choosing Strong Verbs

Make the sentences below more interesting by adding some strong action words (verbs). Cross out each underlined word and write a stronger word above it. You may use words from the following list or think of your own words.

pounded	roared	raced	smashed	soared	streaked	gobbled
yelled	drifted	sailed	shot	gulped	shouted	blasted

1. The car <u>went</u> around the track.

2. Max <u>said</u>, "Help! The house is on fire!"

3. The balloon <u>rose</u> over the treetops.

4. The hungry boy <u>ate</u> his food.

5. The batter <u>hit</u> the ball over the fence.

6. The boat <u>moved</u> over the water.

7. His heart <u>beat</u> wildly.

Using Different Words

A. Your writing will be more interesting if you don't use the same words over and over. On the lines below, list some verbs that you could use instead of "went." The first line has been started for you.

Went on foot hiked _____

Went in a car _____

Went in a boat _____

Went in an airplane _____

Went in a hurry _____

Went slowly _____

Went away from _____

B. The paragraph below uses "went" over and over. Cross out each "went" and write another verb above it. Use a verb from the list you made above or think of a better verb.

Kim and her father went on an exciting trip. First, they went on an airplane to Denver. When they got there, they rented a car and went into the mountains. Then they went on foot to a camp deep in the woods. From there, they went down a river in a canoe. The most exciting part of the river trip was when they went over some rapids. When they came to the end of the river trip, they went in a special bus back to the Denver airport. At last, the happy but tired travelers went home.

Choosing the Exact Word

Try to think of words that mean exactly what you want to say. Exact words will make your writing clearer and more interesting. Read the sentences below. Replace the underlined words with exact words. The first sentence has been done for you.

1. The ~~animal~~ lion roared loudly.

2. The <u>man</u> was in handcuffs.

3. We bought food at the <u>store</u>.

4. The <u>food</u> was cold and sweet.

5. The <u>movie</u> was about Mickey Mouse.

6. The red <u>flower</u> was pretty, but it had thorns.

7. Sam and his dad shot the rapids on a rubber <u>boat</u>.

8. We spent our vacation in a <u>little house</u> in the mountains.

WRITER'S WORKSHOP

Choose words that are STRONG and EXACT. Don't use the same words over and over.

✓ Look at your book report again. Try to make it more interesting by replacing some nouns with exact nouns. If you have used a verb like "went" or "see" over and over, replace that word with a different one. Try to choose words that make your book report clearer and more interesting.

PROOFREADING/PUBLISHING:
Checking Your Book Report

Proofreading is an important step when you are writing. It means to read your book report (or other writing) for mistakes in spelling, grammar, punctuation, or capitalization.

When you PROOFREAD, check your writing carefully for mistakes in spelling, grammar, capitalization, and punctuation.

Here are some marks called PROOFREADING MARKS. You can use them to make changes right on your first draft. That way, you won't have to copy your paper over and over.

Use the caret∧ to show where you need to add a word or two. It works ∧this.
^{like}

✗ means to delete (take out) the punctuation mark, letter, or word that the ✗ slices through. The mark can be used to take out an extra punctuation mark,, a letter like thish, or a whole ~~word~~ word.

◯ means to move the circled word or words to the arrow. It (this) works like.

¶ means to start a new paragraph the next time you copy the paper. The new paragraph should begin right after the ¶ .

A.   Below is part of the book report about Amber Brown. The writer has changed it by using proofreading marks. (If you use a wrong word, it is fine to cross it out and write the correct word above it.)

¶ One afternoon, Amber starts giggling when the ~~teecher~~ *teacher* tells her to

put her head on the desk. Brandi ~~giggeles~~ *giggles*, too, and soon they both

have detention. After that, they start doing fun *things* together. Brandi tells

Amber how hard it was to make ~~frends~~ *friends* when she was a new kid in

school. Even though she tried to be best friends with Hannah,

Hannah was often mean. Brandi and Amber decide that they will

always be ~~niec~~ *nice* to new kids in class, even if they become best friends.

B.   Below are some sentences from the book report about the Iroquois. There are seven mistakes. Find them and correct them by using proofreading marks.

Today the Iroquois live reservations in Wisconsin and Canada. There are museums, there that shoe how the Iroquois lived long ago. Some Iroquois are are farmers and mechanics.. Some go college and to become teachers, doctors, lawyers, and engineers. Iroquois construction workersk have helped build towers and skyscrapers.

A Final Check

When astronauts get ready to blast off, they use a checklist to make sure everything in their spaceship is the way it should be. Now you will use a checklist to be sure that your book report is "A-OK." Use the checklist on the next page to check your report. Put a check mark in the box beside each statement if it is true of your book report. If you can't honestly put down a check mark, go back and make some more changes in your report. Then use the checklist again.

Content

My introduction is interesting. □

My introduction names the book and its author. □

The body of my book report includes a summary. □

I have used details and examples in the body. □

My conclusion is strong and interesting. □

My conclusion tells why someone else should read the book. □

Paragraphs and Sentences

Each of my paragraphs about facts has a main idea. □

My sentences about events are in the proper order. □

I have avoided short, choppy sentences. □

I have joined thoughts together with the best conjunction. □

I have begun every sentence with a capital letter. □

I have ended every sentence with a . ! or ? □

I have indented all my paragraphs. □

Words

I have used strong, exact words. □

I have avoided using the same word over and over. □

I have spelled my words correctly. □

☑ When you're sure your book report is as good as you can make it, copy it neatly on a clean sheet of paper. Remember to use your best handwriting.

W ITING INSTR CTIONS

PREWRITING: Choose and Narrow a Topic

All of us have learned to do some special things. Maybe you can teach a dog to do a trick. Maybe you can cook an egg until it's done just right. Or maybe you can shoot baskets better than anyone else on the block. Can you do any of the things below?

Hang a picture?   Feed a cat?   Build a birdhouse?

Brush a dog?   Make a paper airplane?   Give directions?

Think of some more things you can do. Look at each item in the list below. Then fill in the blank that follows it.

A game I'm good at: _____

Something I can fix: _____

A chore I know how to do: _____

A food I can prepare: _____

A place I know how to find: _____

Something I can build: _____

A trick I can do: _____

Other things I can do: _____

_____

_____

Most of us want to learn to do new things. We might want to plant a cactus without getting stickers in our fingers. Or maybe we'd like to know how to cook pancakes. Make a list of some things you would like to learn to do.

_____

_____

_____

How can you learn to do new things? Sometimes a friend or adult might show you. Sometimes you have to learn things by yourself. Often you will learn by reading INSTRUCTIONS.

WRITER'S WORKSHOP

INSTRUCTIONS are steps you follow in order to make or do something. It's easier to understand and remember instructions that are clear. It's also more fun to read instructions that are interesting.

List some activities you've learned to do by reading instructions.

_____

_____

_____

☑ Using these lessons, you will learn to write clear, interesting instructions. This will help you share something you know how to do. Look at what you wrote on these two pages. Put a check mark by three or four of the activities that interest you most.

Choosing and Narrowing a Topic

Melissa's big brother, Mike, can't cook many things. But he makes the WORLD'S BEST PEANUT BUTTER AND JELLY SANDWICH. Melissa and her friends are always asking him to make some.

One day Mike said, "All right. I'm going to write some instructions. After that, you're on your own. If you want peanut butter and jelly sandwiches, you make them."

Mike decided to write about making peanut butter and jelly sandwiches because that was something he could do well. He wanted to share what he could do with others. "Making Peanut Butter and Jelly Sandwiches" would be Mike's TOPIC.

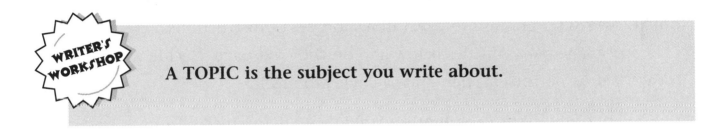

WRITER'S WORKSHOP

A TOPIC is the subject you write about.

Choosing Your Topic

Today you will choose an activity that you like and know how to do. Look back at the lists you made in the first lesson. Choose one of the activities you listed on page 30. Be sure it's one that you like very much and you know how to do. The more you know about this activity, the easier it will be for you to write about. Write the topic you have chosen in the space below:

TOPIC: _____

Narrowing Your Topic

After you choose a topic, ask yourself these questions: Does my topic include too much information for a short set of instructions? Could I write about a smaller part of my topic?

For example, think of all the steps that go into building a birdhouse:

1. buying lumber
2. gathering tools
3. cutting out the parts
4. putting the parts together
5. painting the birdhouse

Any of the five steps in building a birdhouse would be a big job by itself. Maybe a better choice of topic would be "Painting a Birdhouse." Now the topic is NARROW enough to cover in a short set of instructions.

Look at the pairs of titles below and on the next page. Decide which topic in each pair is narrower. Then draw a circle around it.

1. Taking Care of My Baby Brother Waldo

   Feeding Peas to Baby Waldo

2. Animals I Have Known

   How Chris the Cat Chases a Gnat

3. Seven Ways to Pep Up a Birthday Party

   How to Pep Up a Birthday Party with Balloons

4. Putting on a Clown Face

   How to Have a Circus on a Vacant Lot

5. Playing Street Games

   Playing Stickball

6. Rainy-Day Activities

   Playing Checkers

✓ Look at the topic you wrote on page 31. Think about all the steps you will have to write. It could be that the topic you chose is already narrow. Perhaps you could narrow it even more. If you can narrow it, write your new topic here.

NEW TOPIC: _____

NARROW your topic so that you don't have too many steps to write about.

LESSON 2

PREWRITING: Using the Right Materials and Listing the Right Steps

"Okay, gang," said Mike. "Get ready for the WORLD'S BEST instructions for making a peanut butter and jelly sandwich. Mighty Mike is going to write them for you. But first, he will perform his famous magic act. He will make some kids disappear. Poof! Now clear out of here while I think!"

When the kids were gone, Mike chewed on his pencil a minute. Then he decided on the first step: a list of tools and materials needed to make the sandwich. The materials for a sandwich are called its ingredients.

Pretend that Mike needs some help. Write a list of the tools and ingredients for a peanut butter and jelly sandwich on the lines below. Try to write the exact tool or ingredient. ("Sliced rye" is more exact than "bread." "Table knife" is better than "spreader.")

_____

_____

_____

_____

_____

Below are some names of tools and materials.
Circle the MOST EXACT name in each row.

1. fruit jelly	jelly	grape jelly
2. spreader	table knife	knife
3. lumber	plywood	maple plywood
4. cat bowl	dish	bowl
5. paper	crepe paper	orange crepe paper
6. jigsaw	tool	saw
7. color	scarlet	red
8. music	song	folk song

☑ Think about the activity you chose for your topic. Make a list of the tools and materials needed for that activity. Write their exact names on the lines below.

_____

_____

_____

_____

_____

_____

_____

PREWRITING: Listing All the Right Steps

Mike looked at the list of tools and ingredients he had made. "Next," he thought, "I will write how to use them." Mike wrote all the steps for making a peanut butter and jelly sandwich. The first step is at the top, but some of the others are out of order.

Think of the order in which you make a peanut butter and jelly sandwich. Find the second step below and put a 2 in the blank beside it. Continue until you've numbered all the steps correctly.

__1__ If you are right-handed, hold a slice of bread in your left hand and a table knife in your right.

_____ Put the second slice of bread on top of the one that is spread with peanut butter and jelly.

_____ Using the knife, spread one or two tablespoons of peanut butter on the bread.

_____ If you are using crunchy peanut butter, use a light touch when you spread it.

_____ Spread the jelly on top of the peanut butter. If you spread it on the second slice of bread, it will soak in.

_____ Spoon out the same amount of jelly as you used peanut butter.

Using Chronological Order

Instructions are always written in the order in which things actually happen. This is called CHRONOLOGICAL ORDER. Sometimes chronological order is called TIME ORDER. The first thing that happens is written first. The second thing is written second, and the last thing is written last. If you've written or numbered your steps correctly, it will be easy to write them in chronological order.

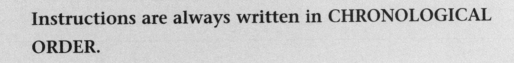

WRITER'S WORKSHOP

Instructions are always written in CHRONOLOGICAL ORDER.

Read the paragraphs below. Put a C in the blank beside the paragraph that is written in chronological order.

_____ To make hot chocolate, mix together cocoa, sugar, and milk in a heavy pan. Put the pan on the stove and heat the mixture slowly. Stop when it is hot, but not boiling. Pour the hot chocolate into a cup and add a marshmallow.

_____ When it is time to give your dog a bath, the first step is to catch him. Before you do that, though, you should have the bathwater, soap, and brushes ready. Hold the dog firmly and dunk him in the water. It usually is best to wear a raincoat.

✓ Now think of the steps for the instructions you have decided to write. Write the steps. If you can, write them in the proper order. It is more important, however, to write them before you forget them. If you write a step out of order, use the blanks to number your steps correctly.

PREWRITING: Getting Ready to Write

It's almost time to write your first draft. Before Mike started writing, he looked back at his list of steps. (See page 36.) Then he grouped the steps together in a way that made sense. Each group of steps told about one part or SUBTOPIC of Mike's topic. Each subtopic would become a paragraph.

Here are the subtopics for Mike's paragraphs. He decided on his subtopics by grouping his steps, then adding a beginning and ending.

Paragraph One: Introduction
Paragraph Two: Gathering Ingredients and Tools
Paragraph Three: Spreading the Peanut Butter
Paragraph Four: Spreading the Jelly
Paragraph Five: Conclusion

Look back at the list of steps *you* wrote on page 38. See if you can decide how to divide your instructions into groups. Each group of steps will become a paragraph. Write the subtopics of your paragraphs on the lines below. Paragraph One should be your introduction and your last paragraph should be your conclusion. (You may not need all the lines.)

Paragraph One: _____

Paragraph Two: _____

Paragraph Three: _____

Paragraph Four: _____

Paragraph Five: _____

Paragraph Six: _____

Practicing Beginnings

Mike made a list of steps to include in his instructions for making a peanut butter and jelly sandwich. He put the steps in the right order and grouped them in subtopics. Then he started writing his first draft.

First, he wrote some beginning sentences that seemed to fit the instructions he had in mind. Then he asked his friend, Mario, to give his opinion of them. Below you will see some of Mike's beginning sentences. Underneath each sentence is Mario's comment.

Some Possible Beginnings

1. Making a peanut butter and jelly sandwich is fun.

   COMMENT: _This sentence isn't very exciting. Besides, who said making a sandwich is fun?_

2. This is how to make a peanut butter and jelly sandwich.

   COMMENT: _This is a clear statement of the topic, but it is boring._

3. It sounds like an ordinary thing to eat, but a well-made peanut butter and jelly sandwich is almost a work of art.

   COMMENT: _This is interesting but long. If you use it, you should explain how a sandwich is like a work of art._

4. A well-made peanut butter and jelly sandwich is no accident.

   COMMENT: _This is clear, short, and interesting. It could be the best of all._

Writing Your Beginning

Now write some beginning sentences for *your* instructions. Write several beginnings, and give your opinion of each one. (Or, ask a friend to give his or her opinion.) Be as honest as you can.

1. _____

_____

COMMENT: _____

2. _____

_____

COMMENT: _____

3. _____

_____

COMMENT: _____

4. _____

_____

COMMENT: _____

✔ Choose the beginning you like best. Write it on another sheet of paper.

DRAFTING: Writing the First Draft

You're on your way! You've written your first sentence. Now it's time to build that sentence into a beginning paragraph. Here is the INTRODUCTION that Mike wrote:

A well-made peanut butter and jelly sandwich is no accident. To make the world's best, you need the right tools and ingredients. You also need a few tips on how to put them together.

Mike's beginning paragraph does two things. First, it captures the reader's attention with an interesting sentence. (Underline that sentence.) Then it "announces" the rest of the paper.

Mike's second paragraph will be about tools and ingredients. (Put brackets [ ] around the sentence that announces that subtopic.) Mike's third and fourth paragraphs will be about making the sandwich. (Put a + before and after the sentence that announces those paragraphs.)

☑ Finish the beginning paragraph of your first draft on your own sheet of paper. Use the beginning sentence you wrote in the last lesson. Then add some other sentences that announce the subtopics of your paper. Skip lines as you write so that you will have space to make changes later.

Writing the Body

You've already decided on the paragraphs for the BODY of your instructions. Now it's time to write those paragraphs.

Here is the first draft Mike wrote for the body of his instructions. Some words are misspelled and there are some other errors. Can you find them? Mike will correct them later.

> Begin by collecting the ingredients. Most people like sliced white bread. Use crunchy or smooth peanut butter, depending on which you like better. A clear fruit jelly like blackberry or grape is better than a jamm that's full of seeds. Have a table knife, a spoon for the jelly, and a plate to put you're sandwich on. Unscrew all the lids.
>
> Hold a slice of bread in your left hand if you're right-handed and a knife in you're right. Spread one or two tablespoons of peanut butter the bread. If you are using crunchy peanut butter, use a light touch as you spread the peanut butter.
>
> Spoon out as much jelly as you used peanut butter. Spred the jelly on top of the peanut butter. If you put it on the second slice of bread, it will soke in.

☑ Write the first draft of your body of instructions. Write it on your sheet of paper under the beginning paragraph. In your body, write one paragraph for each of the subtopics you listed on page 41. Remember to write your ideas in the order you've decided will work best.

WRITER'S WORKSHOP

A FIRST DRAFT is a writer's first try at writing something. The purpose is to get your ideas on paper. Don't worry if you make a few mistakes. You will have a chance to fix them later.

Writing a Conclusion

Mike wanted to write an ending that Melissa and her friends would enjoy. Here is his CONCLUSION:

> Now put the lid on, and prepare to enjoy. What if the peanut butter sticks to the roof of your mouth? That just makes the sandwich last longer.

☑ Write your conclusion on your first draft, right under your body. Try to think of an ending your readers will enjoy.

REVISING: Improving Your Instructions

Mike looked at the instructions he had written. He thought they were pretty good. Then he remembered his promise to write instructions for the WORLD'S BEST sandwich. He decided to try to make his instructions better.

Mike began to REVISE his first draft. Mike changed some things because he thought the new way sounded better. He corrected mistakes as he noticed them.

> **WRITER'S WORKSHOP**
>
> **Writers make improvements and corrections when they REVISE their work.**

Mike made his changes right on his first draft. Here is one of Mike's paragraphs with the changes he made.

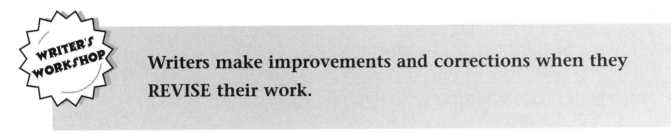

If you're right-handed, hold a slice of bread in
~~Hold a slice of bread in your left hand if you're~~
your left hand   your
~~right-handed~~ and the knife in ~~you're~~ right. Spread
                                              on
one to two tablespoons of peanut butter ʌ the bread.
        spreading
If you are ~~using~~ crunchy peanut butter, use a
              to avoid tearing the bread.
light touch ~~as you spread the peanut butter.~~

45

Using a Checklist

Here is a checklist to help you decide what changes to make in your paper. You may need to go through your paper several times to check all the items. Correct mistakes in spelling and grammar as you see them. Make your changes right on your first draft. When your paper becomes too messy to work with easily, make a new copy.

First Draft Checklist	Yes	Could Be Better
Is the information clear? Can a friend understand and follow my instructions?		
Are my instructions written in correct chronological order?		
Is my beginning interesting? Does it announce the subtopics of my paper?		
Are my instructions in the body interesting?		
Will my readers enjoy my ending paragraph?		
Is each of my paragraphs about one subtopic? Does every sentence of a paragraph fit into its subtopic?		
Can I choose a title that will catch the reader's attention?		

Writing a Title

Write three or four titles that would fit your paper.

_____

_____

_____

_____

☑ Choose your favorite title and add it to your first draft.

Writing Clearly

Are my instructions clear? That is the most important question to ask yourself about your paper. Instructions that aren't clear can cause trouble.

Below are some sentences that aren't clear. After each sentence is a question to help you discover *why* the sentence is unclear. Then the sentence has been written again, with a blank space. Fill in the blank to make each sentence clearer. The first sentence has been done for you.

1. Stir the taffy until tan and bubbly.

   (Until *who* or *what* is tan and bubbly? The cook or the taffy?)

   Stir the taffy until _____it_____ is tan and bubbly.

   (who or what?)

2. Fasten a tail to the kite. It should be long and narrow.

   (*What* should be long and narrow? The tail or the kite?)

   Fasten a _____ _____ tail to the kite.

   (what kind of?)

3. He noticed a hole in the tire, which was large and ragged.

   (*What* was large and ragged? The tire or the hole?)

   He noticed a _____ hole in the tire.

   (what kind of?)

4. Carry sand with a bucket. This should be two inches deep.

   (*What* should be two inches deep? The sand or the bucket?)

   Carry sand with a bucket. _____ should be two inches deep.

   (use a noun)

5. Rock the baby until falling asleep.
   (Until *who* falls asleep? The baby or the one who rocks?)

   Rock the baby until _____ falls asleep.
                          (use a pronoun)

6. When you are giving your dog a bath, a raincoat should be worn.
   (*Who* should wear the raincoat? You or the dog?)

   When you are giving your dog a bath, _____ should
   wear a raincoat.   (use a pronoun)

✓ The best way to make sure your instructions are clear is to ask a friend
to read them. If your friend can follow your instructions, you know they are
clear. (This works best if your friend doesn't already know how to do the
activity you are describing.) If the friend can't understand some of your
instructions, rewrite the parts that aren't clear.

REVISING: Using Transition Words

Mike improved his instructions by adding some TRANSITION WORDS. Transition words are words and phrases that link ideas together. They are like bridges from one paragraph or sentence to another. Here are some examples. (The transition words are underlined.)

Mike made a list of tools and ingredients. <u>After that</u>, he wrote down all the steps for his instructions.

Kim began to build his birdhouse. <u>First</u>, he found some lumber in the garage.

Maria stirred the bubbling taffy. <u>In the meantime</u>, the other children put butter on some plates.

Below are some lists of transition words:

1. *Words That Mention Time*

when	at the same time	then
next	in the meantime	before
finally	first, second, third	after that

2. *Words That Show an Idea Will Be Added*

in addition	and	also

3. *Words That Show a Big Change in Thought*

but	however	yet
even though	on the other hand	still

WRITER'S
WORKSHOP

Use TRANSITION WORDS to link ideas together.

Using Transitions

Fill in the blanks with transition words. Choose words or groups of words from the lists on page 49. Each blank has a number under it. Choose transition words for that blank from the list with the same number. The first one has been done for you.

1. We bought two pounds of apples. <u>In addition</u>, we
   (2)
   bought a dozen oranges.

2. Wet your hair with warm water. _____ massage
   (1)
   about a capful of shampoo into your hair _____ rinse well.
   (2)

3. It is going to rain today. _____ tomorrow should be sunny.
   (3)

4. Let the cake cool for about an hour. _____ ,
   mix up some icing.   (1)

5. We found the badminton set in the attic _____ cleaned it up for the
   (2)
   picnic. _____ we filled the cooler with food.
   (1)

6. I don't play soccer very well. _____ I am a good cheerleader.
   (3)

7. Sam loves to play checkers. He is _____ learning to play chess.
   (2)

✓ Look at your paper again. Can you make it easier to understand by adding some transition words? If you can, make the changes on your first draft.

PROOFREADING/PUBLISHING:
Checking Your Instructions

The last step in writing instructions is to give them one final check. Use the checklist below to look over your first draft. Be sure you are pleased with your writing and the content of your paper.

Content

Are my instructions clear? ☐

Are my instructions written in the right order? ☐

Is my paper interesting? ☐

Does my beginning capture the reader's attention? ☐

Correct Writing

Does each paragraph include only one subtopic? ☐

Have I used clear transitions? ☐

Is each paragraph indented? ☐

Are all my words spelled correctly? ☐

Does each sentence begin with a capital letter? ☐

Does each sentence end with a . ! or ? ☐

☑ Check your first draft again for mistakes in spelling, grammar, or sentence structure. Then write your final copy neatly on a clean sheet of paper.

WRITING A REPORT

PREWRITING: Choosing a Topic

Reviewing the Steps of a Report

You have written a report about an animal. Do you remember the steps you went through in writing that report? Let's review them:

1. You chose your topic. (You picked an animal to write about.)
2. You gathered information from books, encyclopedias, magazines, the Internet, and other sources.
3. You took notes from your sources.
4. You planned your report by writing an outline.
5. You wrote a draft of your report.
6. You revised and proofread your report.

Reports are a very important kind of writing, so you will write another one. This time, you will go through the same steps in writing about a topic of your choice.

Choosing a Topic

The first step is choosing a topic. You can choose a topic based on a favorite hobby, sport, author, or other interest. What interests you? What would you like to know more about? Write down two ideas here.

_____

_____

Another way to choose a topic is to think about what you have been studying in other subjects. Did something you studied in History or Science really grab your interest? In Art or Music, did you meet a painter or composer you'd like to know more about?

Here are some topics you might have studied in your other courses.

Science	History	Art
tropical rain forest	Roman gladiators	Leonardo da Vinci
coral reef	Christopher Columbus	Michelangelo
woolly mammoth	Ferdinand Magellan	Pieter Brueghel

Whatever topic you choose, make sure it is not too broad or too narrow. For example, a student named Ali remembered that he liked learning about Ancient Egypt. But "Ancient Egypt" is too broad a topic for a short report. Ali narrowed "Ancient Egypt" to a topic he could write about. He decided to write about mummies in ancient Egypt.

Freewriting

You can try freewriting to help you think of a topic for your report. When you freewrite, you write down as many thoughts and ideas as you can. You don't have to worry about grammar or spelling. You can just write lists of words.

Try to keep writing for at least three minutes. You can use the space below for your freewriting.

Here are some things I would like to know more about:

_____

_____

_____

_____

_____

_____

_____

Now review your freewriting. Use a highlighter or colored pencil to mark the two topics that interest you most.

Talk with an adult about those two topics. Which one interests you most? Which would you like to write about?

Fill in the blank:

The topic for my report is _____

_____

PREWRITING: Finding Sources for the Report

Now that you have decided on a topic, you need to find sources of information about your topic. At the library, you can look for encyclopedias, books, and magazines. You can also search the Internet.

Searching for Sources at the Library

At the library, use the computer catalog or card catalog to search for sources on your topic. Ask the librarian for help if you need it.

As you find sources that look useful, make a list of them. Follow these rules:

1. Write the title, the name of the author (if it is given), and the numbers of the pages you read.
2. Write B after the source if it is a book, M if it is a magazine, and E if it is an encyclopedia.
3. If the source is a magazine, be sure to write down its date.

Here are some examples:

Title	Author (if given) or Date	Pages
Mummies Made in Egypt (B)	Aliki	3-12
New Book of Knowledge —M (E)		128-131
National Geographic World (M)	April, 1998	9-11

List your library sources here:

Title	Author (if given) or Date	Pages
_____	_____	_____
_____	_____	_____
_____	_____	_____
_____	_____	_____
_____	_____	_____
_____	_____	_____
_____	_____	_____

Searching the Internet

With the help of an adult, you can also search the Internet for information on your topic.

The Internet has a lot of information, but you have to be very careful to be sure you are getting good information.

When you find a reliable source with good information, write down the name of the site, the URL (the Internet address) of the specific page or pages you use, and the date you visit the site. For example:

Name of Site: _Diggin' Up the Facts About Archaeology_

URL: _http://tq.junior.thinkquest.org/5751/mummies.htm_

Date: _November 15, 2002_

List your Internet sources here:

Name of Site: _____

URL: _____

Date: _____

Name of Site: _____

URL: _____

Date: _____

Name of Site: _____

URL: _____

Date: _____

PREWRITING: Organizing the Facts

Choosing Subtopics

As you read your sources, you will find that some facts belong together in subtopics. A subtopic is a group of facts about one special part of a topic.

While reading about mummies, Ali decided on these subtopics:

1. What mummies are

2. How mummies were made

3. Why the ancient Egyptians made mummies

As you read your sources, look for two or three subtopics. These will probably be the points that come up most often in your sources.

When you have decided on your subtopics, write them on the lines below.

1. _____

2. _____

3. _____

Taking Notes

Now it's time to take notes on note cards. Try to write at least two note cards for each of your subtopics. Remember these rules:

1. At the top of each note card, write the subtopic the notes are about.

2. Only write notes about one subtopic on each card.

3. Don't copy from your sources. Put the facts in your own words.

Here is one of Ali's note cards for his report on mummies:

Why the ancient Egyptians ma...

What mummies are

How mummies were made

dried out body with natron (like baking soda)

wrapped body in long strips of linen cloth

removed organs and put them in jars

stuffed body with sand, sawdust, natron

took almost 70 days to make a mummy

PREWRITING: Making an Outline

You organized the information for the report you wrote about an animal by making an outline. Now you will make an outline for this report.

In your outline, use a Roman numeral for each subtopic. Use a capital letter for each fact under the subtopic.

Here is part of the outline Ali wrote for his report on mummies.

II. How mummies were made
    A. removed organs and put them in jars
    B. dried out body with natron (like baking soda)
    C. stuffed body with sand, sawdust, natron
    D. wrapped body in long strips of linen cloth
    E. took almost 70 days to make a mummy

Write the outline for your report on the lines below and on the next page or on a separate sheet of paper.

_____

_____

_____

_____

_____

DRAFTING: Writing the First Draft

You have finished much of the work on your report. Now it's time to use that work to help you write the main part of your report. You will work on the introduction and the conclusion in the next lesson.

Each subtopic in your outline will become a paragraph in your report. Remember, the TOPIC SENTENCE in a paragraph tells what the paragraph will be about. It is usually the first sentence and it states the main idea of the paragraph. Then the rest of the sentences in the paragraph add facts and information about the main idea.

Look again at this part of Ali's outline:

II. How mummies were made
   A. removed organs and put them in jars
   B. dried out body with natron (like baking soda)
   C. stuffed body with sand, sawdust, natron
   D. wrapped body in long strips of linen cloth
   E. took almost 70 days to make a mummy

Ali's subtopic is listed beside the Roman numeral II: "How mummies were made." This subtopic is the main idea of one paragraph in Ali's report. Ali decided to write it as a question:

How did the ancient Egyptians make mummies?

Ali then turned each fact in his outline into a sentence to support the main idea. Here is the paragraph:

How did the ancient Egyptians make mummies? First they removed the main organs, like the heart and liver, and put them in jars. Then they dried out the body by covering it with natron. Natron is like baking soda. After the body was dry, they stuffed it with sawdust, sand, and natron. Then they wrapped it in long strips of linen cloth. It could take almost 70 days to finish making a mummy.

✓ Using your notes and your outline, write a draft of the main part of your report on a sheet of paper. Write a paragraph for each subtopic in your outline. Double-space when you write, so that it will be easy to go back and make revisions.

DRAFTING: Writing the Introduction and Conclusion

Writing the Introduction

When you wrote the first paragraph for your report on an animal, you did two things. You told your reader what the report was about, and you wrote an opening that would interest your reader.

There are different ways to interest a reader. For example:

1. You can begin with an interesting fact: "Imagine a tongue that is more than a foot long!"
2. You can begin with a question: "Did you ever wonder who catches the ants for the anteaters in the zoo?"

When Ali sat down to write his introduction, he thought about how the movies show mummies. Here is what he wrote:

"Eeeek!" A woman screams. She runs from the monster. It looks like a dead man wrapped in ragged bandages. It's a *mummy!* But mummies only walk in movies. Real mummies aren't scary, but they are very interesting. Let's find out about what mummies are, how they were *made,* and why the ancient Egyptians made them.

64

Now you try writing an introduction on another sheet of paper. Remember, your introduction should do the following things:

1. Catch the reader's interest
2. Tell what your report is about

Double-space when you write so that it will be easy to go back and make revisions.

Writing the Conclusion

Your conclusion should let your reader know the paper is ending. It should leave your reader with the feeling that the report has been neatly wrapped up. Your conclusion can be a sentence at the end of the last paragraph, or it can be a separate paragraph.

In your conclusion, you should not introduce any new ideas or topics. Look at this draft of a conclusion that Ali wrote for his report on mummies. Cross out the sentence that Ali should remove from his conclusion.

So, mummies are not monsters at all. They were very important to the ancient Egyptians. And they still interest us today. Sometimes the Egyptians even made mummies of their pets!

Read through the draft of your report. Pay special attention to the last paragraph and the last sentence. Does it seem to end the paper, or does the writing just seem to trail off?

Now try writing a conclusion that brings your report to a satisfying close. Double-space when you write so that it will be easy to go back and make revisions.

Revising the Report

You have written a complete draft of your report, from beginning to end. Now you can take a look at the whole report and think of ways to make it even better.

Reading Aloud

Read your draft to an adult. As you read, you may notice sentences you want to change or take out, or you might see where you need to add more information. If you see places to change or improve the writing, make a mark on the draft, and then continue reading aloud. Then go back to the passages you have marked and revise the draft.

A Revision Checklist

☑ After you have revised your report, go back over it one more time. Use this checklist to help you. As you finish each item, check it off.

The Introduction

_____ Does my first paragraph catch the reader's interest?

_____ Does my first paragraph tell what the report is about?

The Middle

_____ Is each paragraph about one idea?

_____ Does the first sentence in each paragraph state what the paragraph will be about?

_____ Do I have enough facts in the paragraph to tell about the main idea?

_____ Are there sentences that do not tell about the main idea that I should take out?

The Conclusion

_____ Does the last sentence or paragraph make a good ending for the report?

Write a Title

Now try to think of a good title for your report. Like an introduction, a title should catch your reader's interest and tell what the report will be about.

Try writing two or three possible titles here. Which one works best? Write that one at the top of your draft.

_____

_____

_____

Proofreading and Publishing the Report

This is the last step! Before you make your final copy, look once more at the revised draft of your report. This time, look at the details. Use this checklist to help you. As you finish each item, check it off.

_____ Are all the words spelled correctly?

_____ Does each sentence begin with a capital letter?

_____ Do names of people and places begin with a capital letter?

_____ Does each sentence end with the correct punctuation mark?

_____ Does each sentence make sense?

When you have made all the corrections to your report, make a clean copy. Write very carefully so that you don't introduce any new mistakes. Make sure to write the title of the report at the top of the first page, along with your name and the date.

Share your finished report with family and friends.

PREWRITING: Reading a Story

The Long-Haired Eyewok

It was just after dark. Children were hurrying home for dinner. They chattered excitedly about the play they were presenting. In the cold dark night they thought they saw shadowy things behind buildings. Every bush or light pole seemed scary.

The children weren't imagining things. Lurking behind a bush was a long-haired eyewok. His seven yellow eyes watched the children walk by. The eyes turned and wobbled on rubbery stems around his head as he noticed some children still on the playground. They were shooting baskets, trying to get in one more game before it was too dark.

The long-haired eyewok started toward them. His eyes lit up like seven little flashlights. The long fur on his body swished as he walked. He didn't make a sound. Though his feet were quite large, they were very soft.

Just as he got to the playground, the children saw him. They screamed and yelled and ran away. "I'm just not good at making friends," Harry said.

At home, Harry told his eyewok uncle about all the times he had tried to make friends. "They always run and scream. No one wants to be friends with a monster."

Uncle Fred looked at a poster he had found on a pole. "I think I may have an idea," he said. His yellow eyes blinked as he thought out his plan. "Tonight I will have a surprise for you." He told Harry his plans.

After Harry had done his monster chores, Uncle Fred sent him back out into the darkness. He walked to the community center. Soon he was standing at the door. "Well, here goes!" he said. He burst through the door and shouted, "Hello, everyone!"

Instead of screaming, there was silence. Everyone was staring at Harry. "Take your place on the stage, everyone!" a tall woman announced. "Our *Space Invaders* show is about to begin."

"Neat costume!" whispered a green, slimy space creature, looking at him through her mask. "How did you make the eyes light up?" Soon Harry was surrounded by many aliens, monsters, and space warriors.

"Could you help me with my costume?" someone asked. "Can you come to my house tomorrow?" Everyone wanted to play with the kid in the best costume.

"Thank goodness," thought Harry. "I hope this play lasts forever!"

What you have just read is a story. It didn't really happen. You knew that the story was make-believe, didn't you? How did you know?

_____

_____

_____

_____

_____

Make-believe stories belong to a kind of writing called FICTION. Fiction includes make-believe books, movies, plays, and television programs. Fiction tells about make-believe happenings as if they were true.

Problems in Stories

The people, animals, or make-believe beings in a story are called its CHARACTERS. Many stories are about PROBLEMS that characters face. These stories tell how the characters tried to solve their problems.

A. Here are some problems that happened in stories. Draw a line from each problem to the name of the story in which it happened.

A little girl gets blown to a strange land by a windstorm. More than anything, she wants to get home to Kansas.

Winnie-the-Pooh

Three homebuilders have trouble with a character who wants to blow in their houses and eat the homebuilders for dinner.

The Three Little Pigs

A bear eats too much and gets stuck in a rabbit hole.

The Wizard of Oz

Three early morning hikers learn that someone has broken into their home.

The Three Bears

B. Use the lines below to describe the problem that Harry had in "The Long-Haired Eyewok."

_____

_____

_____

_____

_____

_____

C. Here are some problems that could be turned into stories:

1. Two boys borrow their uncle's boat and get stranded on an island.

2. A bored girl digs a pond in the backyard. Her mother falls in.

3. An earth child builds a rocket. By accident, he blasts off his dog to the rooftop.

4. A monster wants to ride on the city bus. But he doesn't have exact change and no one will change his monster money.

5. A girl wants to own a dog, but her brother is allergic to dog hair.

D. Choose one of the problems above that you think would make a good story. Or, if you like, make up some problems from your own imagination. Write your ideas on the lines below. The problems you list can be real problems that bother you. Or, they can be make-believe problems that are silly, scary, or exciting.

1. _____

_____

_____

_____

2. _____

_____

_____

_____

☑ Choose the problem you think would make the best story. You may choose one that you thought up, or one of the five problems given above. Put a star beside the problem you choose. Later on, you will turn the problem into a story that other people can read.

PREWRITING: Getting to Know the Characters of a Story

Every story has CHARACTERS. Characters are the WHO of a story—the people, animals, or make-believe creatures in the story.

A story without characters would be like an empty island. Nothing much would happen. Each character has a special part to play in the story. The character may cause the story's problem, solve it, or make the problem easier or harder. The main character is usually the one who faces the problem.

Here are some characters from stories you might know. On the line beside each character, tell about the special part the character played in a story.

1. Charlotte, in
   Charlotte's Web
   _____
   _____

2. The wolf in "The
   Three Little Pigs"
   _____
   _____

3. Harry in "The
   Long-Haired Eyewok"
   _____
   _____

4. Uncle Fred in "The
   Long-Haired Eyewok"
   _____
   _____

Getting to Know Your Characters

Writers need to know some things about their characters before putting them in stories. They need to know how the characters LOOK, SOUND, and ACT.

A good way to start getting to know characters is to give them names. Names can sometimes tell us something about a character. Look at the list of characters' names below. Decide what each name might tell you about the character.

Pippy _____

Pigpen _____

Scrooge _____

Lord Skrallwinch _____

✓ Of course, not every name tells something about the character. Some characters are named "Sam" or "Maria." Use these lines to list a few characters you might use in your story. (Think about the problem you chose on page 72. What characters would you need in a story about that problem?)

1. _____

2. _____

3. _____

4. _____

5. _____

6. _____

Writers sometimes use CHARACTER BOXES to help them develop their characters. Of course, the writers make up the facts they put in the boxes. Here is one example:

Name	Looks Like	Sounds Like	Acts Like
Harry	scary monster; long fur; seven yellow eyes on stems	a human child	a lonely child; keeps trying to make friends

✔ Use the character boxes below to describe the characters for your story. List their names in the first column. Then tell how you think your characters would look, sound, and act.

Name	Looks Like	Sounds Like	Acts Like

PREWRITING: Identifying the Plot of a Story

The PLOT is the plan for the story. It tells what happens. At the beginning of the story, the characters are identified. Usually, there is a problem that has to be solved.

The characters try to solve their problem in the middle of the story. Sometimes they don't get the problem solved and have to try again.

By the end of the story, the problem is usually solved. We also find out how the characters feel now that the problem is solved.

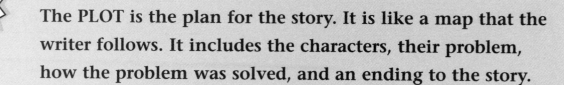

The PLOT is the plan for the story. It is like a map that the writer follows. It includes the characters, their problem, how the problem was solved, and an ending to the story.

✓ You have identified the characters and the problem you want to write about in your story. Think about how the characters might solve the problem. List some possible solutions on the lines below.

1. _____

2. _____

3. _____

4. _____

5. _____

Planning the Most Exciting Part

Here is a list of the things that happen in "The Long-Haired Eyewok."

1. The eyewok walks to the playground.

2. The children see him and run.

3. Harry tells his uncle about his problem.

4. Uncle Fred has an idea.

5. Harry goes to the community center and bursts through the door.

6. The tall woman tells him to take his place on stage.

7. The kids want to play with him.

Some stories follow special patterns. One pattern for a plot is called the A-frame. It looks like this:

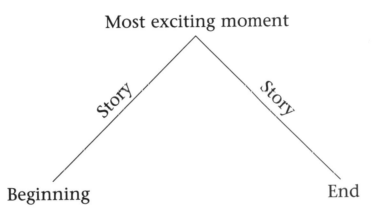

Most exciting moment

Story   Story

Beginning   End

Some writers try to build the excitement in their stories until they reach the MOST EXCITING MOMENT at the top of the A-Frame. Then they let the story slide down the other side of the A-Frame to the end.

The first step is to decide on the most exciting moment. What do you think is the most exciting moment in "The Long-Haired Eyewok"? Did you say when Harry bursts through the door? That's when you wonder if Uncle Fred's plan will work.

Here is an A-frame for "The Long-Haired Eyewok." The beginning has been filled in. Fill in other happenings that make up the plot. Put the most exciting moment at the top.

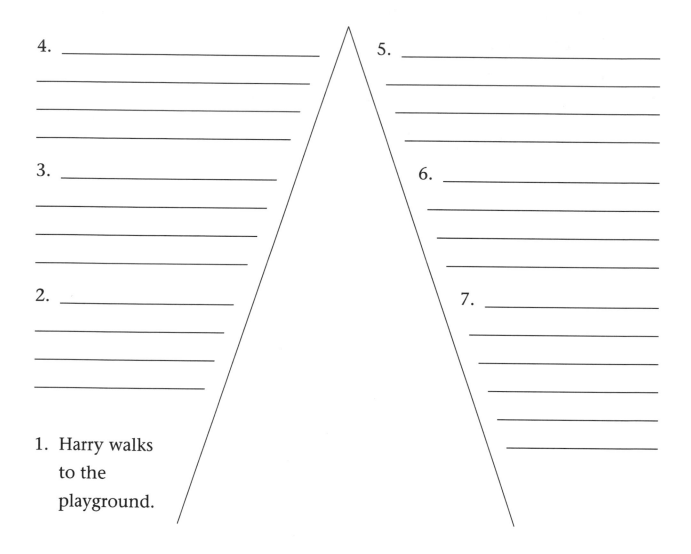

4. _____
   _____
   _____
   _____

3. _____
   _____
   _____
   _____

2. _____
   _____
   _____
   _____

1. Harry walks
   to the
   playground.

5. _____
   _____
   _____
   _____

6. _____
   _____
   _____
   _____

7. _____
   _____
   _____
   _____
   _____
   _____

☑ Make a list of the things that could happen in the story you are going to write. Use the problem and the characters you have chosen. What might happen in the beginning of the story? How will the problem be identified? What happens next? How will the problem be solved?

DRAFTING: Describing the Setting of a Story

By now, you have chosen the characters and the plot for your story. You also need to think about the time and place in which the story will happen. That time and place make up the SETTING.

You know what is going to happen in your story and you know who it is going to happen to. Now you must decide when and where it is going to happen. When will your story take place—in the present, the past, or the future? If it's in the past, how long ago? If it's in the future, how far ahead?

Where will your story take place? This is an important decision. It can help set the mood of the story.

The dark, scary street in "The Long-Haired Eyewok" is just right for a monster story. But that story also has two other settings. Look at the story again and see if you can find them. Describe them on the lines below.

First setting: <u>dark, scary street</u>

Second setting: _____

Third setting: _____

The SETTING is where and when a story takes place.

A. Here is a list of settings. Pick two and describe what kinds of things you would expect to see in each one.

an old, creaking house	the moon
a crowded street	an underground burrow
a dark, lonely road	a tree house
a forest	a grocery store
a farm	a fire station
a toy store	a school
an island	a shoe
a spaceship	a passenger train
a doll's house	a dungeon

B. Think of a setting that would be good for each of the stories described below. Write it on the line beneath the idea for the story. Or, if you like, choose one of the settings listed above and write it on the line.

1. Two dolls come to life and play tricks on their owner.

____

2. A friendly ghost picks up after a messy child.

____

3. A rabbit and a chipmunk become friends.

____

4. Two children quarrel on the way to a picnic.

____

C. You can use a SETTING BOX to help you plan the settings for your story. The box can help you see how your setting will look in the mind of the reader. Look at the setting box for "Red Riding Hood" at the top of the next page. What words are used to describe things?

Place	Looks Like	Special Sounds in the Place
a path in the woods	tall trees, wildflowers, small animals scampering, dirt path	birds tweeting, rustling leaves, footsteps, child humming

D. Use this setting box to plan a setting for your story.

Place	Looks Like	Special Sounds in the Place

Writing Your First Draft

You have chosen a PROBLEM to write about in a story. You have picked out and named your CHARACTERS. You have worked out a PLOT and described a SETTING. Now it is time to write the first draft of your story.

Don't expect to write a perfect story on the first try. Just follow your plot and do your best. You will have a chance to add details to your story later. Skip lines as you write so that you can make changes later.

✓ Look again at the list of happenings in your story. Begin by introducing your characters. Describe the setting. Identify the problem. Try to make the story more and more exciting until it reaches its most exciting moment and the problem is solved. Then write an ending.

REVISING: Improving Your Story

The Story in Review

Fill in the blanks to review what you've learned about writing a story.

1. A plan for WHAT happens in a story = _____ .

2. The WHO of a story = _____ .

3. WHERE and WHEN a story happens = _____ .

You have thought of a plot, characters, and a setting. You have used them to write a story. Now it is time to begin improving your story. When the first draft is finished, writers go to work again. They change things to make their stories more interesting or exciting.

Here is the first draft of the opening paragraphs of "The Long-Haired Eyewok." Compare this draft to the final version of the story on page 69. What improvements did the writer make?

It was just after dark. Children were hurrying home for dinner.

They talked about the play they were presenting. In the cold dark

night they thought they saw things behind buildings.

The children weren't imagining things. A long-haired eyewok was

behind a bush. His seven yellow eyes watched the children walk by.

The eyes turned around his head as he noticed some children still on

the playground. They were shooting baskets, trying to get in one

more game before it was too dark.

Make Your Story Come Alive with Details

One way you can improve your story is to add some details about things that happen. Have you ever read a story so interesting that you forgot where you were? Or what was happening around you? The story probably made you feel that way by describing events with great care. The writer chose just the right details to catch your imagination.

Describing events is an important part of every story. Here is a paragraph from *The Mouse and the Motorcycle* by Beverly Cleary. Underline words (look for action verbs) that tell at least four things that happen in the paragraph.

Pb-pb-b-b-b. Ralph picked up his tail and started the motor. Without taking time to let it warm up, he gunned it with all the breath he could inhale. The motorcycle got off to a faster start than Ralph expected, so fast that Ralph lost control. He shot out from under the bed just as the vacuum cleaner died with a long drawn-out growl.

✓ All those things happened in just a few seconds. Look back at the first draft of your story. Can you add some details about events that will make your story "come alive" for the reader? Write some of your ideas on the lines below or on the draft of your story.

1. Event: _____

    Details: _____

    _____

2. Event: _____

    Details: _____

    _____

REVISING: Appealing to the Senses

Describing with All Five Senses

The long-haired eyewok started toward them. His eyes lit up like seven little flashlights. The long fur on his body swished as he walked. He didn't make a sound. Though his feet were quite large, they were very soft.

The paragraph above tells you how the long-haired eyewok looked. The writer has tried to make you see pictures in your mind as you read the words. Do you? Underline the words in the paragraph that help you see how the eyewok looked.

But seeing is just *one* of our senses. Writers also try to make us hear, feel, smell, and taste things in our imagination as we read their stories. The paragraphs below will give you some examples:

The smells from the deli were sweet and spicy. They made Andy feel hungry as he walked by the door. He found a smashed corn chip in his pocket, but it tasted like paper. Maybe it wasn't such a good idea to run away before lunch.

How could so many people be in such a hurry? Andy felt lonely, even though he was surrounded by people. The blaring horn of a battered yellow cab made him jump. He leaned against a building, but even the bricks were unfriendly. They felt rough and cold against his hand. Andy thought for a minute. Then he turned around and headed back home.

Look back at the paragraphs about Andy's walk through the city. Then fill in the blanks below. Use words from the paragraphs that describe things that Andy could see, hear, taste, smell, or touch.

See _____

Hear _____

Taste _____

Smell _____

Touch _____

WRITER'S WORKSHOP

Writers choose words that help us to know how things look, sound, feel, smell, or taste.

Using Adjectives and Adverbs

ADJECTIVES are words that describe nouns. Adjectives help readers see pictures in their mind.

Add some adjectives to the nouns below so that they make word pictures. The first one has been done for you.

_____ tiny cluttered _____ room

_____ snake

_____ robot

_____ day

_____ sunset

ADVERBS can also help you draw word pictures for your readers. Adverbs are words that describe verbs. Use your imagination to fill in the blanks below with adverbs. The first one has been done for you.

1. The frightened child screamed __wildly_____ .

2. The star was shining _____ .

3. The man spoke _____ .

4. Ann drove the car _____ .

5. The boat rocked _____ .

Now add some adjectives and adverbs to the first draft of the story you are writing. Try to make your readers see pictures in their mind.

Another Kind of Word Picture

Writers have another way to make word pictures in their readers' mind. They tell how one thing is like something else that usually seems different. They COMPARE one thing to another. This kind of word picture is called a SIMILE. A simile uses *like* or *as* to compare one thing to another.

The writer of "The Long-Haired Eyewok" used this simile: "His eyes lit up like seven little flashlights." On the blanks below, write the two things that the writer compared.

The light from Harry's _____ is compared with the light from

_____ .

The writer was pretty sure that readers knew how the light from a flashlight would look. So he used that idea to make the reader see the light made by Harry's eyes.

Finish the sentences below by telling how one thing is like another. Try to think of similes that will make word pictures in a reader's mind.

1. The boy ran around the room like _____ .

2. The girl walked down the street like _____ .

3. The boat sank in the lake like _____ .

You also can compare things *without* using the word "like." You can say "My father was a bear when he saw the broken window." What you mean is "My father acted like a bear." But you let your reader imagine your father as a bear. This kind of word picture is called a METAPHOR.

Finish the sentences below.

1. Your room is _____

_____ .

2. My dog is _____

_____ .

3. The playground is _____

_____ .

4. The boy is _____

_____ .

☑ Make at least one word picture in the first draft of your story by comparing one thing with another. Use either a simile or a metaphor.

REVISING: Writing Conversations

"The fact is," said Rabbit, "you're stuck."

"It all comes," said Pooh crossly, "of not having front doors big enough."

"It all comes," said Rabbit sternly, "of eating too much."

In these lines from *Winnie-the-Pooh* by A. A. Milne, Rabbit and Pooh are having a CONVERSATION. Of course, rabbits and bears don't talk as people do, except in stories. When you are writing a story, all of your characters can speak like people. Even if they are animals, or trees, or cars and trucks, their conversations can sound like those of people.

There are two signs that tell us someone is speaking in a story. One sign is the use of a word like "said." Can you think of the other sign? (Look at the conversation at the top of this page.) Yes, the QUOTATION MARKS tell us that someone is speaking. Did you notice that the commas and periods are INSIDE the quotation marks?

WRITER'S WORKSHOP

In stories, each speech by a character begins and ends with QUOTATION MARKS. Punctuation marks like . , ! and ? go inside the quotation marks.

If you look closely, you will find another rule about conversation in stories. The rule is: a new paragraph begins every time a different character starts to speak. If a writer doesn't begin a new paragraph for each new speaker, readers will get confused. They won't know who is saying what.

A NEW PARAGRAPH begins each time a different character starts speaking.

Conversations can tell us what a character is like. Below are some exact words of characters from stories. Draw a line from each speech to the character you think would have made the speech.

"Get on your horse, cowboy. There ain't room here for another hand!"   An astronaut

"But, Mother!" begged Nancy. "I'll have time to do my chores after the movie!"   A ranch owner

"This is Apollo Thirty to Houston. We are firing our retro rockets."   A young girl

Use the lines below to make up a conversation for the characters in the story you are writing. Try to think how the characters would speak. Remember to begin and end each character's words with quotation marks. Begin a new paragraph whenever a different character starts speaking.

_____

_____

_____

_____

_____

☑ If you like, add the conversation you have written to your story.

REVISING: Looking at Beginnings and Endings

The beginning of a story is important. It should make the reader want to go on reading the story. Writers sometimes wait until a story is almost finished to write the beginning. By that time, they know what part of the story will catch the reader's interest.

Here are three ways you can begin your story:

1. by describing a setting or character
2. by quoting something a character says
3. by telling about an event

Below are some examples. After each example, write the number (from the list above) of the kind of beginning it is.

_____ One day Henny-Penny was picking up corn in the cornyard when—whack!—something hit her upon the head.

_____ Sunday afternoon was clear, and the snow-covered prairie sparkled.
(From *These Happy Golden Years* by Laura Ingalls Wilder)

_____ "Exactly what are you boys up to?" demanded Horace Tremayne.
(From *The Mystery of the Magic Circle* by M. V. Carey)

☑ Write a new beginning for your story on the lines that follow. You may describe a character or setting, write a conversation, or tell about something important that happened. If you like your new beginning, add it to your story.

_____

_____

_____

Writing an Ending

The ending of a story is important, too. It is like a period or exclamation mark at the end of a sentence. It tells the reader "this story is finished." It should answer most questions the reader may still have. Here is the ending of "The Long-Haired Eyewok."

"Neat costume!" whispered a green, slimy space creature, looking at him through her mask. "How did you make the eyes light up?" Soon Harry was surrounded by many aliens, monsters, and space warriors.

"Could you help me with my costume?" someone asked. "Can you come to my house tomorrow?" Everyone wanted to play with the kid in the best costume.

"Thank goodness," thought Harry. "I hope this play lasts forever!"

Does that ending make you feel that the story is finished? _____

Does it answer any questions that you had? If so, which ones? _____

_____

_____

☑ Write a new ending for your story. Make sure that your ending is strong enough to make the reader feel "this story is finished!" If any questions still need to be answered, do that in the ending. If you like your new ending, add it to your story.

Also, if you haven't already done so, write a title for your story that will catch your reader's interest.

LESSON 9

PROOFREADING/PUBLISHING: Checking Your Story

Before you make the final copy of your story, use the checklist below to check it over. If you can't put a check in each blank space, make the changes that are needed.

Content *(Plot, Characters, and Setting)*

Does my story follow a plan? ☐

Will my beginning catch the attention of the reader? ☐

Have I told or shown my readers how my characters look, sound, and act? ☐

Have I identified a problem? ☐

Does each character play a special part? ☐

Did I use conversations to help make my characters seem real? ☐

Does my setting fit the story? ☐

Do I describe how the setting looks and sounds? ☐

Did I use adjectives or compare one thing to another? ☐

Is my ending strong? ☐

Proofreading Your Story

Does each sentence begin with a capital letter? ☐

Do the exact words of a character begin and end with quotation marks? ☐

Do I start a new paragraph each time a different character starts to speak? ☐

Does each sentence end with the correct punctuation mark? ☐

Are all of my words spelled correctly? ☐

☑ Write the final draft of your story. You may wish to draw pictures to go with it. Then make a cover with the title on it.